College Reading and Study Skills

Twelfth Edition

KATHLEEN T. McWHORTER
NIAGARA COUNTY COMMUNITY COLLEGE

BRETTE McWHORTER SEMBER

PEARSON

Boston Columbus Indianapolis New York San Francisco Upper Saddle River
Amsterdam Cape Town Dubai London Madrid Milan Munich Paris Montreal Toronto
Delhi Mexico City Sao Paulo Sydney Hong Kong Seoul Singapore Taipei Tokyo

Editor in Chief: Eric Stano
Senior Acquisitions Editor: Nancy Blaine
Development Editor: Erin Reilly
Marketing Manager: Kurt Massey
Senior Supplements Editor: Donna Campion
Executive Digital Producer: Stefanie A. Snajder
Digital Project Manager: Janell Lantana
Digital Editor: Rob St. Laurent
Production Manager: Ellen MacElree
Project Coordination, Text Design, and Electronic Page Makeup: PreMediaGlobal
Cover Design Manager: John Callahan
Cover Designer: Kay Petronio
Cover Image: Erik Degraaf/Veer
Senior Manufacturing Buyer: Dennis J. Para
Printer and Binder: Quad/Graphics/Dubuque
Cover Printer: Lehigh-Phoenix Color/Hagerstown

This title is restricted to sales and distribution in North America only.

For permission to use copyrighted material, grateful acknowledgment is made to the copyright holders on pp. 504–507, which are hereby made part of this copyright page.

Lexile® is a trademark of MetaMetrics, Inc., and is registered in the United States and abroad. The trademarks and names of other companies and products mentioned herein are the property of their respective owners. Copyright © 2011 MetaMetrics, Inc. All rights reserved.

Library of Congress Cataloging-in-Publication Data

McWhorter, Kathleen T.
  College reading and study skills / Kathleen T. McWhorter, Brette McWhorter Sember. — 12th ed.
    p. cm.
  ISBN-13: 978-0-205-21302-3
  ISBN-10: 0-205-21302-2
  1. Reading (Higher education) 2. Study skills. I. Sember, Brette McWhorter, 1968- II. Title.
  LB2395.3.M386 2011
  428.4071'2—dc23

                                                                                    2011045838

10 9 8 7 6 5 4 3 2 1—QGD—15 14 13 12

Student ISBN-13: 978-0-205-21302-3
Student ISBN-10:   0-205-21302-2

AIE ISBN-13: 978-0-205-21731-1
AIE ISBN-10:   0-205-21731-1

CONTENTS

BRIEF CONTENTS

Across eleven editions, *College Reading and Study Skills* has demonstrated that reading and study skills are inseparable. A student must develop skills in each area in order to handle college work successfully. With this goal in mind, I have tried to provide complete coverage of both reading and study skills throughout and to show their relationship and interdependency. In doing so, my emphasis has been on direct instruction. My central aim is to teach reading and study through a how-to approach.

NEW TO THE TWELFTH EDITION

The primary thrust of the revision is to build a text that recognizes and accommodates visual learners and thinkers, emphasizes new forms of classroom communication, and recognizes that students need guidance in learning from textbooks and other academic sources effectively. Specific changes include the following:

NEW USING COLLEGE TEXTBOOKS SECTIONS. Using textbook excerpts from a wide range of disciplines, this section guides students in integrating and applying the skills taught in each chapter to their other courses.

NEW VISUAL THINKING ACTIVITIES. These new activities prompt students to think analytically about visuals. In chapters devoted to study skills, *Visual Thinking: Applying Skills* photos ask students to consider the skill they are learning in that chapter in light of the visual. In reading skills chapters, *Visual Thinking: Analyzing Images* photos prompt students to explore an image and the purpose it serves in relation to a reading passage.

NEW THEMATIC READINGS. Part Five of the book contains 9 readings, grouped according to three themes. Theme A on body adornment returns to this edition. A new Theme B raises controversial issues having to do with genetics. Finally, Theme C on the Internet and technology addresses the implications of Web 2.0 and social networking.

NEW SUCCESS WORKSHOPS. The college classroom is changing, and students need new skills to meet the challenges of increasingly visual, electronic, and collaborative school and work environments. To meet this need, new Success Workshops titled "Read and Think Visually," "Manage Your Electronic Life," and "Communicate and Network with Other Students" have been added.

NEW FULL-LENGTH TEXTBOOK CHAPTER. The twelfth edition features a full-length sample chapter titled "Emotion and Motivation" from an introductory psychology text, allowing students an opportunity to apply skills taught throughout the text to actual textbook material.

NEW LEARNING GOALS. Listed at the beginning of each chapter, new objectives appear as a numbered list and correspond to the major headings in the chapter. At the end of each chapter, revised "Self-Test Summaries" provide students with an opportunity to test themselves on their mastery of these learning goals.

UPDATED TEXTBOOK SELECTIONS FOR EXERCISES. All selections have been checked for reading level; many have been replaced with excerpts from the most up-to-date editions of textbooks.

NEW ANNOTATED INSTRUCTOR'S EDITION.   For instructors, the Annotated Instructor's Edition is an exact replica of the student text with answers provided on the page.

NEW LEXILE MEASURES.   A Lexile® measure is the most widely used reading metric in U.S. schools. Lexile measures indicate the reading levels of the longer selections in the Annotated Instructor's Editions of all Pearson's reading books and the reading level of content in MyReadingLab. See the Annotated Instructor's Edition of (text) and the Instructor's Manual for more details.

CONTENT OVERVIEW

College Reading and Study Skills, Twelfth Edition, presents the basic strategies for college success, including time management, analysis of learning style, active reading, and note taking. The text offers strategies for strengthening literal and critical comprehension, improving vocabulary skills, and developing reading flexibility. Students also discover methods for reading and learning from textbook assignments, including outlining and summarizing, and for taking exams. The reading and study skills I have chosen to present are those most vital to students' success in college. Each unit teaches skills that are immediately usable—all have clear and direct application to students' course work.

Because I believe that critical thinking and reading skills are essential to college success, these skills are emphasized in the text. I introduce students to critical thinking skills by explaining Bloom's hierarchy of cognitive skills early and then showing their academic application throughout the text. *College Reading and Study Skills* offers direct skill instruction in critical reading and includes key topics such as making inferences, asking critical questions, analyzing arguments, and evaluating Internet sources.

The units of the text are interchangeable, which enables the instructor to adapt the material to a variety of instructional sequences.

SUCCESS WORKSHOPS.   Appearing at the beginning of each part, the Success Workshops use a fun, lively, and accessible format to provide students with skills that will directly and immediately contribute to their college success. Topics include acclimation to the college environment, academic image, concentration, stress management, and reading and thinking visually.

PART ONE: BUILDING A FOUNDATION FOR ACADEMIC SUCCESS.   This section provides an introduction to the college experience and presents skills, habits, and attitudes that contribute to academic success. Chapter 3 in this section establishes the theoretical framework of the text by discussing the learning and memory processes and the principles on which many of the skills presented throughout the text are based.

PART TWO: READING AND THINKING CRITICALLY.   This section focuses on the development of reading skills for both textbooks and other common academic reading assignments. Critical thinking and reading skills are emphasized. Students are shown methods of learning specialized vocabulary and discover systems for vocabulary learning. Techniques for reading graphics are presented. Critical thinking topics in Chapter 9 include making inferences, distinguishing between fact and opinion, recognizing tone, and analyzing arguments. Chapter 10 focuses on evaluating an author's techniques. Reading and evaluating electronic sources, including how to adapt reading strategies for online and other sources and how to avoid cyberplagiarism, are discussed in depth in Chapters 13 and 14.

PART THREE: READING TEXTBOOK CHAPTERS AND ASSIGNMENTS.   These chapters teach skills that enable students to learn College Textbook assignments. Chapter 15 focuses on how to highlight and mark a textbook. Chapter 16 teaches students to organize information using outlining, summarizing, and mapping.

PART FOUR: STRATEGIES FOR ACADEMIC ACHIEVEMENT.   The purpose of this section is to help students prepare for and take exams. Organizing for study and review, identifying what to study, and methods for review are emphasized. Methods of learning through writing—paraphrasing, self-testing, and keeping a learning journal—are described. Students learn specific strategies for taking objective tests, standardized tests, and essay exams, as well as for controlling test anxiety. In Chapter 20, students learn to adjust their reading rate to suit their purpose, the desired level of comprehension, and the nature of the material they are reading.

PART FIVE AND SIX: THEMATIC READINGS AND SAMPLE TEXTBOOK CHAPTER. This section contains 9 readings, grouped according to three themes: body adornment (sociology/cultural anthropology), controversies in science (biology/genetics), and technology and the Internet (media studies/business). These readings, which represent the kind of texts that may be assigned in academic courses, provide students with an opportunity to apply skills taught throughout the text. Finally, a sample textbook chapter taken from an introduction to psychology college text, titled "Emotion and Motivation," allows students to work with actual textbook material to apply skills taught throughout the text. The chapter is representative of college textbooks and of the learning aids they contain. An "Understanding Your Textbook" quiz following the chapter tests students' familiarity with the learning aids contained in the chapter.

SPECIAL FEATURES

The following features enhance the text's effectiveness and directly contribute to students' success:

- **Learning Style.** The text emphasizes individual student learning styles and encourages students to adapt their reading and study techniques to suit their learning characteristics, as well as the characteristics of the learning task.
- **Reading as a Process.** This text emphasizes reading as a cognitive process. Applying the findings from the research areas of metacognition and prose structure analysis, students are encouraged to approach reading as an active mental process of selecting, processing, and organizing information to be learned.
- **Metacognition.** Students are encouraged to establish their concentration, activate prior knowledge, define their purposes, and select appropriate reading strategies prior to reading. They are also shown how to strengthen their comprehension, monitor that comprehension, select what to learn, and organize information. They learn to assess the effectiveness of their learning, revise and modify their learning strategies as needed, and apply and integrate course content.
- **Skill Application.** Students learn to problem-solve and explore applications through case studies of academic situations included at the end of each chapter. The exercises are labeled "Applying Your Skills." "Discussing the Chapter" questions ask students to reflect on how the advice in the chapter will work in their assignments. "Analyzing a Study Situation" questions present students with mini-cases and ask them how to best approach an academic challenge. Finally, "Working on Collaborative Projects" exercises provide opportunities for group work.
- **Learning Experiments/Learning Principles.** Each chapter begins with an interactive learning experiment designed to engage students immediately in an activity that demonstrates a principle of learning that will help students learn the chapter content. The student begins the chapter by doing, not simply by beginning to read.
- **Visual Literacy.** A new Success Workshop titled "Read and Think Visually" introduces students to the basics of visual literacy, while "Visual Thinking" activities in each chapter encourage students to think critically about visuals.
- **Chapter Learning Goals and Additional Practice on MyReadingLab.** Each chapter opens with chapter learning objectives that correspond to the major headings in the chapter. Suggested click paths through MyReadingLab lead to activities related to major headings.
- **Chapter Focus and Purpose Questions.** The first section of each chapter opens with a question that models the question students commonly ask before beginning an assigned chapter: Why should I learn this? Following each question are several answers that establish the importance and relevance of the skills taught in the chapter.
- **Interactive Assignments.** The Success Workshops and the learning experiments at the beginning of each chapter engage students and function as interactive learning opportunities.
- **Writing to Learn.** The text emphasizes writing as a means of learning. Writing-to-learn strategies include paraphrasing, self-testing, outlining, summarizing, mapping, and keeping a learning journal.

- **Realistic Reading Assignments.** Exercises often include excerpts from college texts across a wide range of disciplines, providing realistic examples of college textbook reading. Furthermore, new "Using College Textbooks" sections guide students in making the most of their textbooks.
- **Thematic Readings.** Nine readings, grouped according to three themes, are contained in Part Five. These readings provide realistic materials on which to apply skills taught in the text. They also provide students with an essential link between in-chapter practice exercises and independent application of new techniques in their own textbooks, and valuable practice in synthesizing and evaluating ideas.
- **Self-Test Chapter Summaries.** Linked to the chapter's learning goals, the chapter summaries use an interactive question–answer format that encourages students to become more active learners.
- **Quick Quizzes.** A multiple-choice quick quiz is included at the end of each chapter. Each quiz assesses mastery of chapter content, provides students with feedback on their learning, and prepares students for further evaluation conducted by their instructor.
- **Visual Appeal.** The text recognizes that many students are visual learners and presents material visually, using maps, charts, tables, and diagrams.
- **Using Technology.** The text offers students advice for using technology to make their study habits more effective. See "Tech Support" boxes throughout the text.

THE TEACHING AND LEARNING PACKAGE
Book-Specific Ancillary Materials

- **Instructor's Manual/Test Bank.** This supplement contains teaching suggestions for each chapter along with numerous tests formatted for easy distribution and scoring. It includes a complete answer key, strategies for approaching individual chapters, a set of overhead projection materials, and suggestions for integrating the many Pearson ancillaries. The Test Bank portion of the supplement includes content-based chapter quizzes and mastery tests to enable students to apply skills taught in every chapter. ISBN: 0-205-21732-X.
- **Annotated Instructor's Edition.** This supplement is an exact replica of the student text with answers provided. ISBN: 0-205-21731-1.
- **PowerPoint Presentations.** A presentation for each chapter, which is structured around the chapter learning objectives, can be downloaded at Pearson's Instructor Resource Center. You can use these presentations as is or edit them to suit your lecturing style. ISBN: 0-205-21721-4.
- **MyReadingLab.** This Web site is specifically created for developmental students and provides diagnostics, practice tests, and reporting on student reading skills and reading levels.
- **Expanding Your Vocabulary.** Instructors may choose to shrink-wrap *College Reading and Study Skills* with a copy of *Expanding Your Vocabulary*. This book, written by Kathleen McWhorter, works well as a supplemental text providing additional instruction and practice in vocabulary.

ACKNOWLEDGMENTS

In preparing this edition, I appreciate the excellent ideas, suggestions, and advice provided by reviewers: Kathy Barker, Grays Harbor College; Shawn Bixler, Summit College; Joan Lippens, Washtenaw Community College; Janet Michalak, Niagara County Community College; Betty J. Perkinson, Tidewater Community College; Mary Lee Sandusky, Kent State University at Trumbull; Ann Thomas, Dekalb Tech; Hollie Van Horne, Kent State University/Salem Campus; and Carla Young, CCAC–Allegheny Campus.

The editorial staff at Pearson deserve special recognition and thanks for the guidance, support, and direction they have provided. In particular I wish to thank Erin Reilly, my development editor, for her valuable advice and assistance and Nancy Blaine, acquisitions editor, for her enthusiastic support of the revision.

KATHLEEN T. MCWHORTER
www.pearsonhighered.com

SUCCESS WORKSHOP

1 Learn Everything You Can in the First Week

Your first week of classes and your first week on campus are some of the most important days you will ever spend.

Discovering . . .
What Your Courses Require

When you accept a new job, your manager spends time explaining your job and its responsibilities. These first few days are important because you learn what is expected and what you must do to earn your paycheck. The first few days of a college course are equally important. You learn what your instructor expects and what you must do to earn a grade and receive credit for the course. Often, much of this information is contained in a course syllabus—a handout distributed on the first day or in the first week of class. Look and listen for the answers to the following questions.

Course objectives: What are you expected to learn in the course? (Pay particular attention to these; exams measure your ability to achieve these objectives.)

Course organization: How is the course structured? What portions will be lecture, conferences, discussion, small group work, and so forth?

Exams, quizzes, and assignments: When are exams scheduled, and what assignments are due? (Record dates for each in a pocket calendar.) What are the penalties for late assignments? Are make-up exams offered?

Grading system: How will your grade be determined? How much does each test or assignment count?

Class participation and attendance: What are your instructor's policies regarding attendance? Is class participation part of your grade?

Office hours: Where is your instructor's office, and what hours is he or she available?

If any of this information is not provided during the first week of class, be sure to ask your instructor.

Analyzing . . .
Your Course Syllabi

Examine the syllabus for each of your courses. Identify the course objectives and course organization. Highlight or underline the schedule for assignments, quizzes, and exams. Then immediately transfer these dates into your calendar. After your first week of classes, go through your calendar, noting the due dates for the next month. Begin now to plan how you will schedule your time to meet your due dates.